The 5-Minute Self-Love Journal

The 5-Minute SELF-LOVE JOURNAL

Prompts, Practices, and Affirmations
for Greater Self-Compassion
and Self-Acceptance

Tiffany Shelton Mariolle, PhD

**ROCKRIDGE
PRESS**

First Rockridge Press trade paperback edition 2022

Rockridge Press and the Rockridge Press logo are trademarks or registered trademarks of Callisto Media Inc. and/or its affiliates in the United States and other countries and may not be used without written permission.

For general information on our other products and services, please contact our Customer Care Department within the United States at (866) 744-2665, or outside the United States at (510) 253-0500.

Paperback ISBN: 978-1-68539-745-6

Manufactured in the United States of America

Interior and Cover Designer: Jake Flaherty
Art Producer: Megan Baggott
Production Editor: Jax Berman and Ellina Litmanovich
Production Manager: Lanore Coloprisco

10 9 8 7 6 5 4 3 2 1 0

This journal belongs to

Introduction

Congratulations! You are embarking on a beautiful self-love journey. Welcome to an opportunity to cultivate more self-love with a simple journaling practice. My name is Dr. Tiffany Shelton Mariolle, and I am a licensed psychologist who specializes in helping people live more meaningful lives. Through a combination of neuropsychology, coaching, and writing, I strive to help people truly enjoy the journey of life. More specifically, helping my clients increase self-love has helped them experience more joy, stress less, and find more meaning in life. In my work with clients, it became evident that obstacles like inner criticism, insecurity, guilt, and even shame were impeding my clients' ability to fully experience joy. Self-love is a journey, not a destination. It is a practice that, if continually cultivated, can offer us peace, confidence, and a sense of freedom. For example, I've seen self-love help clients align with a greater sense of purpose and live more fulfilled lives. I've seen how self-compassion has helped some clients become more accepting, enabling them to work on their problems more authentically. And perhaps most rewarding, I've seen how the journey of increasing self-kindness has helped many clients feel happy with who they are.

This journal offers exercises that take no more than five minutes to complete. Each entry provides an opportunity to practice self-love with a journal prompt, practice, and affirmation. The great thing about this journal is that you can choose how best to use it. You may choose to work through it from start to finish, or you may select a particular entry that speaks to you each day. How you use the book is up to you.

Journaling is a fantastic practice for increased mental well-being and happiness. However, this strategy should not be used as a substitute for professional treatment. Ongoing mental health symptoms, such as depression or anxiety, should be treated by a licensed professional (i.e., a psychologist, psychiatrist, or medical doctor). Reaching out to a professional for support is something to be celebrated because it is the first and most important step in your commitment to improving!

I'm beyond excited to be a part of your self-love journey. You deserve to live a life fully in love with who you are. May this journal help you experience more kindness, compassion, and acceptance for yourself.

ACCEPT YOURSELF
AS YOU ARE

Accepting yourself involves finding ways to silence your inner critic. What situations usually trigger your inner critic to activate?

_____

_____

_____

_____

_____

_____

The next time you find yourself in one of these situations, say to yourself: "I do not have to be perfect. I'm more than enough."

I boldly accept and embrace every single part of me. I am perfectly imperfect.

UNAPOLOGETICALLY PUT YOURSELF FIRST

Prioritizing yourself is key to self-love. Make a list of your favorite ways to care for yourself—mind, body, and soul.

_____

_____

_____

_____

_____

_____

_____

Fill a box with your favorite self-care activities (such as a mindful coloring book, a jump rope, scented lotion, etc.). Then engage in one activity from this kit daily for a week.

Prioritizing my needs helps me show up better for myself and my loved ones.

LEARN TO TRULY
TRUST YOURSELF

Trusting yourself builds confidence. When was the last time you struggled with making a decision or trusting your gut?

_____

_____

_____

_____

_____

_____

The next time you have a choice to make, practice making decisions quickly. Consider the information at hand without going back and forth for too long. Remind yourself that you have done your best with the information you have.

I can trust my intuition. My mistakes are my teachers, and my wisdom is my guide.

PROTECT YOUR PEACE AND JOY

Healthy boundaries are rules we establish in relationships that support our well-being while also supporting our growth. For example, you may assert your need to be respectfully spoken to while still being open to constructive feedback. What areas of your life would benefit from more explicit and healthy boundaries?

_____

_____

_____

_____

_____

Become more mindful of feelings of unfairness within relationships and document these moments in a note-taking app. Review your notes regularly to detect themes or opportunities to assert healthy boundaries.

What I need matters, and I have the right to communicate those needs.

LIVE UP TO YOUR VALUES

Living up to your own standards and values cultivates self-respect that supports self-love. What standards are important to you?

_____

_____

_____

_____

_____

_____

Think of an area of your life in which you aren't living up to your own standards. Visualize completely fulfilling your values in this life domain.

I am honest and live with integrity. I strive to live according to my highest values.

LEARN TO PRACTICE
SELF-RESPECT

Respecting yourself means treating yourself with dignity and high regard. What characteristics do you respect about yourself and why?

_____

_____

_____

_____

_____

Write down five people you highly respect or admire. Note the characteristics and traits you have in common with these individuals. Review this list of shared values frequently and assess what you are doing to embody these values.

Receiving respect starts with respecting myself.
I honor myself with dignity and high regard.

TAKE RESPONSIBILITY FOR YOURSELF

There is power in taking ownership of your life. Signs of giving too much of your power away include feelings of helplessness, hopelessness, or self-pity. Are there any parts of your life that you have blamed on other people or circumstances? How could you take more ownership?

_____

_____

_____

_____

_____

The next time you feel the urge to blame others, take a moment to take your power back. Ask yourself, "What part of this situation can I take responsibility for?"

I am the creator of my life and have the power to take responsibility for myself.

ENJOY YOUR OWN COMPANY

Part of cultivating self-love is loving the time you spend with yourself. What are some solitary activities that bring you peace or joy?

_____

_____

_____

_____

_____

_____

Plan an extravagant date to spend entirely with yourself. Try to spend this outing doing an activity that you wouldn't normally do alone but would be exciting to try.

I enjoy the time I spend with myself and indulge in peaceful moments in solitude.

KNOW AND HONOR
YOUR LIMITS

Sometimes, especially in our careers, we push ourselves beyond our limitations without compassion for our well-being. How could you be more compassionate toward your own limitations?

_____

_____

_____

_____

_____

_____

To avoid burnout, develop a list of your personal signs of becoming overwhelmed or fatigued. When you notice any of these signs in the future, evaluate if you are pushing yourself beyond your limits.

**I show myself love by honoring
my limits and capacity.**

BRAVELY SPEAK YOUR TRUTH

You amplify your self-love when you express your own truth. What form of self-expression helps you feel most heard or validated (i.e., talking to a friend, creating art, writing poetry, etc.)? What about these forms of expression resonate with you the most?

_____

_____

_____

_____

_____

The next time you are asked your opinion on something or even how you're doing, practice sharing authentically how you feel.

I courageously tap into my intuition and express my truth. My voice is worthy of being heard.

AUTHENTICALLY YOU

Living an authentic life is a powerful way to show yourself love. When was a time you acted authentically and felt your confidence renewed as a result?

_____

_____

_____

_____

_____

_____

Plan to spend an upcoming weekend prioritizing your own wants and desires. Take this weekend to revel in decisions that make you happy first and foremost.

I am living a life fueled by my own desires and passions. I love my authentic life.

CULTIVATE KINDNESS

Self-compassion fuels self-love. Write about your ability to be kind to yourself. Is this something you struggle with? What makes it difficult?

_____

_____

_____

_____

_____

_____

Write a letter to yourself expressing gratitude for who you are. Write as if you are writing to a friend, lauding them with kindness.

I offer myself kindness, love, and grace.
I am worthy of receiving compassion.

BUILD SELF-ESTEEM
THAT LASTS

When it comes to confidence, what we do has more weight than what we think. What are you doing in your life that you are proud of?

_____

_____

_____

_____

_____

_____

Make a list of actions that would bring you a sense of pride if completed. Then choose one activity from that list to begin this week.

**The more I do things that are estimable,
the more my self-esteem grows.**

GET TO KNOW YOURSELF

Loving yourself starts with knowing who you are, but sometimes we don't take the time to reflect. Brainstorm ways you could spend more time getting to know yourself.

_____

_____

_____

_____

_____

_____

Take five minutes to sit quietly with your eyes closed, becoming the observer of your thoughts. Try to tune in to the fact that your thoughts are not your identity.

Investing time in getting to truly know myself is an act of love.

BE PROUD OF
WHO YOU ARE

You are worth celebrating. What does success mean to you?

_____

_____

_____

_____

_____

_____

Close your eyes and take a moment to reflect on your wins. Think about your successes in life that you are most proud of and notice how it feels to reflect on your success. As you recall victory, notice what emotions, body sensations, and thoughts arise.

I know I have what it takes to be successful, and I am proud of my journey.

BE PATIENT WITH YOURSELF

On your self-love journey, you may struggle with feeling like you are behind in life. Do you ever judge yourself in comparison to others? What prompts you to start comparing yourself?

_____

_____

_____

_____

_____

Make a list of all the things you are grateful for in your own life. Place this list in an area you frequent regularly like a reading nook or in your journal. Read this list whenever you find yourself comparing yourself to others.

I am right on time in my life journey. Everything that is for me will come in due time.

YOU ARE NOT A FRAUD

Imposter syndrome can erode your self-love. Remind yourself that you don't have to be perfect to be qualified. What skills do you have that support your professional work?

_____

_____

_____

_____

_____

_____

When you feel imposter syndrome, take a moment to use this acronym: BAT. This stands for *breathe, accept* your emotions, and *transform* your thoughts with an affirmation.

**I release self-doubt and perfectionism
and embrace confidence.**

PRACTICE BEING EASY ON YOURSELF

A common tactic of our inner critic is being hard on ourselves when we make a mistake. When was the last time you made a mistake and how did you react?

_____

_____

_____

_____

_____

The next time you make a mistake, visualize yourself as a caring parent comforting yourself. Say to yourself what you imagine such a figure would share with their child.

**I'm human and make mistakes.
The key is to learn and grow.**

DON'T LET FAILURE DEFINE YOU

Knowing the difference between falling short of a goal and being a failure will aid your self-love journey. There is no such thing as a failure. Sometimes we fail, sometimes we succeed; all the while we are striving to improve. Write about all the reasons why achievements and failures do not define you.

_____

_____

_____

_____

_____

_____

If you find yourself feeling like a failure, take a moment to reassess the rational reasons you didn't achieve your goal. Then visualize accomplishing the goal with success.

I am more than my successes and failures, and I am worthy of love no matter what.

DISCIPLINE AS SELF-LOVE

Self-discipline is about keeping the promises you make to yourself, and it is an often forgotten form of self-love. What areas of your life could use more discipline?

_____

_____

_____

_____

_____

_____

This week, challenge yourself to be more disciplined by making a promise to yourself and keeping it. Make this promise a simple one that supports one of your goals, such as writing for ten minutes per day.

I owe it to myself to take steps to pursue what I want in life.

CONNECTING WITH
SELF-LOVE IN MIND

The quality of your relationships is a direct reflection of your level of self-love, because in many ways, we teach others how to treat us. Do the relationships in your life reflect the love and respect you deserve?

_____

_____

_____

_____

_____

Make a list of all the qualities of a healthy relationship. Reference relationships you admire and healthy qualities about the current relationships in your life. Brainstorm how you could cultivate these types of relationships going forward.

**My connections and attachments reflect
the tremendous love I have for myself.**

RELEASING BODY STRESS AND TENSION

Taking care of our bodies is an essential self-care practice. Reflect on where in your body you feel stress manifest (such as tension in your shoulders, achy joints, tingling in your fingers, etc.) and brainstorm how you could you relieve that stress.

_____

_____

_____

_____

_____

Resting in a comfortable position, close your eyes and take a moment to release the tension in your body. With each exhale, see if you can energetically sink deeper into your support while relaxing.

**Caring for my body is an act of love and peace.
I compassionately nurture my body.**

LOVE THE BODY YOU HAVE

Sometimes we spend so much time criticizing our bodies, we forget the miracles they do for us. Take time to reflect on all the ways you appreciate your body.

_____

_____

_____

_____

_____

_____

Plan an occasion to show your body some love. Think about what you like; some options include getting a massage, stretching, or eating a delicious meal.

**I love the body I am in. My body is
a miracle in and of itself.**

MINDFULLY ENJOY THE PRESENT MOMENT

The more mindfully we live, the more opportunities we have to consciously love ourselves and the lives we have. When are the times you feel most present in your life?

_____

_____

_____

_____

_____

Use your senses to become present in the moment. For five minutes, as you deeply breathe, notice what your senses are telling you.

**The present moment is the best
time to offer myself love.**

LOVE YOURSELF—MIND, BODY, AND SPIRIT

Holistic self-care can foster lasting self-love because it accounts for your whole self rather than focusing on one aspect of your well-being. Use the space provided to evaluate how well you are taking care of your mind, body, and spirit.

_____

_____

_____

_____

_____

Develop a wellness plan that addresses how you would holistically like to improve your self-care regarding your mind, body, and spirit. Then decide on one small step and start taking action.

I honor my whole self as I radically pursue self-love. I care for myself in mind, body, and spirit.

GET THE SUPPORT YOU NEED

Self-love doesn't mean you have to do everything alone, and professional support can improve your quality of life. What areas of your mental or physical health would benefit from professional help?

_____

_____

_____

_____

_____

Create a resource sheet that includes contact information for the individuals (including professionals) from whom you receive care in your community. If need be, research new professionals to add to your sheet.

My self-love journey doesn't have to be solitary. I deserve support and care.

TAKING CARE OF
YOUR EMOTIONS

Emotional awareness is a great way to practice self-love. Reflect on your past week, and journal about all the emotions you have felt recently.

_____

_____

_____

_____

_____

Resting with your eyes closed, take five minutes to briefly meditate while letting emotions arise. As you breathe deeply and mindfully, notice what emotions arise without holding on to them.

**My emotional experience is worth validating
with kindness and compassion.**

CHECK SELF-DEPRECATING THOUGHTS

Sometimes we can be our own worst critics and think mean thoughts about ourselves without even realizing it. Reflect on what self-deprecating thoughts most commonly show up for you.

_____

_____

_____

_____

_____

The next time you notice that you're reprimanding yourself with a disparaging thought, offer yourself love by placing your hand on your heart and thinking of three kind statements a friend might say to you to counteract your negative self-talk.

In this moment, I offer myself love and cherish who I am.

FOSTER SELF-DEFINITION AND INDEPENDENCE

Defining who you are and embracing your individuality is a beautiful way to offer yourself love. Write about all the things that make you unique.

_____

_____

_____

_____

_____

_____

Practice leaning into your own will and self-determination by setting three goals you would like to accomplish on your own. Reflect on how achieving each goal will foster your independence.

I am committed to defining who I am. I cherish my autonomy and self-determination.

YOU DON'T ALWAYS HAVE TO BE STRONG

On the journey to cultivating self-love, vulnerability is an incredibly useful tool. Write about ways you could allow yourself to be vulnerable in a healthy and safe way.

_____

_____

_____

_____

_____

_____

Prepare a list of people you trust to support you on days you don't feel strong. Refer to this list when you are down, and reach out to someone you feel safe being vulnerable with.

I deserve moments to let my guard down. I can tolerate uncertainty.

PERFECTION, THE ENEMY OF SELF-LOVE

Unrealistic expectations and toxic perfectionism make it hard to accept ourselves completely. Reflect on how you react to your imperfections and flaws.

_____

_____

_____

_____

_____

In an attempt to overcome perfectionism, begin celebrating imperfections. The next time you realize a flaw or imperfection about yourself, take a second to appreciate that imperfection by naming two things that are beautiful about it.

**There is beauty in my imperfections.
I celebrate myself just as I am.**

BEING ENOUGH

Many go-getters mistakenly make loving themselves conditional on their achievements. Do you only offer yourself love when you achieve goals?

_____

_____

_____

_____

_____

_____

Sit down, close your eyes, and take a moment to visualize what it would look like to love yourself unconditionally. Envision what your life would be like with unconditional self-love.

I do not have to do anything to earn my worth. I deserve love just for being me.

KNOW AND HONOR
WHO YOU ARE

The foundation of loving yourself is self-knowledge. Describe your own personality traits and characteristics. How would you describe yourself to a stranger?

_____

_____

_____

_____

_____

_____

Create a version of yourself according to the description you wrote. Use whatever creative outlet speaks to you—draw, sculpt, make music—just be sure to capture what you love about yourself.

**My confidence rises as I consistently
get to know myself.**

TAKE TIME TO THANK YOURSELF

A great way to show yourself love is by taking time to do nice things for yourself. What acts of service could you do for yourself to express your appreciation?

_____

_____

_____

_____

_____

_____

Practice doing something nice for yourself with a refreshing work break. After working for an hour, take a ten-minute, screen-free break to rejuvenate yourself by doing things like stretching, listening to music, or doodling.

I appreciate myself. I will provide myself with the renewed energy and vigor I deserve.

LEARN TO REGULATE YOURSELF

Regulating your emotions helps you feel more confident and in control. This is because emotional regulation gives you the tools to process negative feelings in a productive way, while dysregulation leaves us feeling powerless to our emotions. What are your personal signs of emotional dysregulation?

_____

_____

_____

_____

_____

The next time you feel any negative emotion, take a moment to regulate your breathing. Inhale through your nose like you're smelling a rose, and exhale like you're blowing out a candle.

I am in control of my response to my emotions. I courageously allow emotions to flow through my experience.

USE MOVEMENT
FOR SELF-LOVE

Frequently getting your body moving is physical expression of
self-love. Evaluate your physical activity level, given your abilities,
and determine goals for increased movement if needed and able.

_____

_____

_____

_____

_____

_____

Chest stretches are commonly used to metaphorically promote
self-love. Inhale and hug yourself tight, then exhale and open
your arms out wide. Repeat for one minute.

**I enjoy moving my body. It feels
good to treat my body well.**

LOVE YOURSELF
THROUGH LOSS

After experiencing grief, many people feel like they have lost a piece of themselves. Are there parts of yourself you would like to reconnect to in the wake of loss?

_____

_____

_____

_____

_____

_____

Decide on one thing you can do to move closer to the parts of you that you wrote about. Keep it simple, remembering this is a compassionate first step, not a forceful leap. Do this action before the end of the week.

I offer myself love as I move through loss.
I can find ways to feel whole again.

SET YOURSELF FREE
WITH FORGIVENESS

Holding grudges wastes our energy and fosters resentment. When was the last time you held a grudge against someone, and how were you able to let it go?

_____

_____

_____

_____

_____

_____

Write a letter to someone you feel harmed you. Acknowledge how you feel and what hurt you. Then, symbolically release your resentment by destroying the letter.

I breathe in joy and release resentment.

KNOW THAT YOU ARE LOVE

In many ways, love starts from within. Our true essence, possibly underneath pain or fear, is kindness, compassion, patience, and acceptance. Write about what love means to you and how you embody that definition.

_____

_____

_____

_____

_____

_____

Take five minutes to meditate on yourself as love. As you breathe deeply, repeat in your mind, "I am love."

**Self-love starts with embracing
my loving true essence.**

YOU ARE WORTHY OF LOVE

What are twenty things you truly value about yourself?

_____

_____

_____

_____

_____

_____

_____

Close your eyes and visualize yourself emanating light. For five minutes, as you imagine yourself radiating light, repeat in your mind, "I am worthy."

I value so many things about myself. My worth is inherent and not conditional.

TACKLING NEGATIVE BELIEFS

What beliefs about yourself or the world might you have that are fueling your inner critic?

_____

_____

_____

_____

Use this train exercise to discover additional underlying negative beliefs to empower yourself to change them. Divide a piece of paper into four columns. In the first column, recall the most recent time you felt a negative emotion. In the next column, write down the thoughts you had during this circumstance. In the third column, answer this question to uncover the negative belief: If these thoughts were true, what does it say about me, others, or the world? In the last column, write two statements that refute that negative belief.

I lean into my positive beliefs, and know that I have the power to overcome my negative beliefs.

CHOOSE EASE

Simply put, everything doesn't have to be hard. It's perfectly okay to offer yourself kindness by allowing things to be easy. Are there times you overcomplicate things and put too much pressure on yourself?

_____

_____

_____

_____

_____

_____

The next time you have a project to complete, start with an easy plan. Devise a way to simplify the project as much as possible without losing the desired quality. Ask yourself, "How can I make this easy?"

Choosing ease affirms my ability to love on myself with simplicity, softness, and compassion.

IDENTIFY AND EMBRACE YOUR BLESSINGS

Sometimes, our minds focus more on the negative than the positive. Journal about five things you are grateful for today and how they make you feel.

_____

_____

_____

_____

_____

Label a mason jar "Gratitude Jar." Whenever you feel grateful for something, write it down and add it to the jar. At the end of each month, review the contents of the jar.

I have a grateful heart. Appreciation and gratitude help me love my life and myself more.

LEARN TO GIVE
YOURSELF GRACE

Grace is a great tool for self-love because it includes acceptance and kindness. It works in conjunction with self-discipline for a balanced approach to compassionate growth. What does grace mean to you, and how do you practice it in your life?

_____

_____

_____

_____

_____

_____

Grab an adult coloring page and colored pencils. Allow yourself to freely color for five minutes. Give yourself grace to color outside the lines, letting go of expectations and not judging the outcome of your work.

I deserve grace. I deserve to give myself credit. I deserve to give myself a break.

CULTIVATING PEACE
AND CALM

Creating a peaceful life and avoiding chaos provides a secure foundation for self-love. This is because security offers the freedom that comes with safety and stability. What does having a peaceful life mean to you?

_____

_____

_____

_____

_____

Promote inner peace by practicing stillness. Amid peace and quiet, find a comfortable resting position and close your eyes. Try to sit in stillness for five minutes.

**Calm is my refuge and safety. I lean into
the joy that comes from a peaceful life.**

MINDFUL EATING

Savoring your food with present-mindedness is a way of taking care of yourself that's shown to reduce anxiety and cultivate healthy eating. How would it feel to be more present while eating?

_____

_____

_____

_____

_____

_____

Make a tasty meal for yourself and set aside uninterrupted time to enjoy it. As you eat, stay present with the experience by savoring the flavors and paying attention to your senses.

**I deserve to take time to savor
and appreciate my food.**

ATTUNE TO YOUR BODY

Feeling connected to your body can offer you a sense of ground-edness, a stable foundation for practicing self-love with ease. How connected do you feel with your body?

_____

_____

_____

_____

_____

_____

Take five minutes to stretch your body with chair stretches. Seated, gently stretch out your limbs, torso, and face while mind-fully noticing the sensations in your body.

**Consciously connecting with my body
offers me moments of loving peace.**

CONNECT WITH MOTHER EARTH

Part of self-love can include creating positive experiences for yourself. Connecting with nature has been shown to cultivate positive feelings like peacefulness. What do you feel when connecting with nature?

_____

_____

_____

_____

_____

Take a five-minute mindful nature break today. Find time to go outside and connect with the outdoors. Some ideas include sitting in the grass, bird-watching, or safely sunbathing.

I breathe calmly and cultivate calming experiences for myself.

PROMOTE RESTORATIVE SLEEP

Adequate sleep lays the foundation for optimal physical and emotional well-being. Over the last week, how would you characterize your sleep hygiene and habits?

_____

_____

_____

_____

_____

_____

This week, do this quick practice to promote restorative sleep. Before going to bed, turn off all screens and engage in deep breathing while you close your eyes and visualize yourself sleeping peacefully.

I prioritize restorative sleep that supports my well-being.

LOVING HYDRATION

Staying hydrated is an easy way to show yourself some love. Dehydration has been shown to increase the risk of conditions like depression. Is there room for improvement in your hydration habits?

_____

_____

_____

_____

_____

_____

_____

Fill a jug or pitcher with enough water to hydrate yourself for an entire day. Set a timer to remind yourself to drink every two hours.

I love taking care of myself with healthy habits.

EVERYDAY LUXURY

Restorative practices, such as soothing baths, offer us time to pamper ourselves outside of our normal routines. What reaction do you have to treating yourself?

_____

_____

_____

_____

_____

_____

Indulge in a restorative bath to offer yourself some kindness. Consider setting the scene with aromatherapy candles, bath salts, hot tea, or calming music.

It feels good to treat myself to lavish experiences. I deserve to celebrate myself.

MOTIVATING BREAKS

On the days you feel unmotivated, it can be hard to keep the promises you make to yourself. How do you handle feeling unmotivated? Does it affect your self-esteem?

_____

_____

_____

_____

_____

Use the Pomodoro Technique the next time you are feeling unmotivated: For every twenty-five minutes you work, take a five-minute break. This technique has been shown to boost motivation and productivity.

I can find ways to inspire myself and maintain self-discipline. I motivate myself with compassion and kindness.

THE POWER OF MUSIC

Music has the power to change our mood and make us feel more alive, especially music we love. Make a self-love playlist that makes you feel empowered and self-confident.

_____

_____

_____

_____

_____

_____

Referencing the playlist you made, pick a favorite song to make your "theme song" for a week. Integrate playing this theme song into your morning routine and notice how it makes you feel.

**I have the tools to feel powerful and assured.
Enjoying music is a fun way to show myself love.**

RELEASING CRITICAL THOUGHTS

Critical thoughts impact your ability to love yourself by over-emphasizing perfectionism versus acceptance. What was your most recent critical thought and how did it make you feel?

_____

_____

_____

_____

_____

Begin the work to change your relationship with critical thoughts by practicing the "leaves on a stream" visualization. Imagine each thought written on a leaf floating downstream. As a leaf moves away, allow new thoughts to flow in and out of your mind the same way.

I accept every part of who I am. I do not have to be perfect to deserve love.

DETACHING FROM THOUGHTS

Sometimes the busyness of our minds can cause negative emotions. One way to take care of your mind is to use stillness and detachment to clear it. How can you incorporate more stillness into your life?

_____

_____

_____

_____

_____

Engage in a five-minute candle meditation to promote stillness and healthy detachment from your thoughts. Mindfully observe a lit candle. When you notice a distracting thought, gently refocus your attention on the candle.

I remind myself that thoughts aren't always facts and aren't always helpful. I can choose a new thought to take care of myself.

LEARNING TO
ACCEPT THINGS

The stronger your ability to accept, the easier it will be to radically love yourself. What are three imperfect things that you compassionately accept about yourself?

_____

_____

_____

_____

_____

Practice the skill of accepting things as they are with mindful listening. Take five minutes to sit quietly as you consciously listen to your surroundings without judgment.

Acceptance is a muscle I can strengthen through practice. I will continue to work on accepting every part of me.

USING YOUR SELF-KNOWLEDGE FOR GROWTH

You can use the power of self-knowledge to lovingly develop yourself. Reflect on any aspects of your life experience that you would like to improve.

_____

_____

_____

_____

_____

Your dreams can help you cultivate personal development. Write down the next dream you remember and ponder what you would change about it. Do you notice any insights that can help you grow as a person?

I see myself with clarity. I like what I see while being open to evolving.

FEELING SAFE AND SECURE

If you know how to regulate yourself, you have a powerful tool to promote feelings of safety and security. This can be a beautiful act of self-love when you are feeling anxiety. What helps you feel calm when you experience worry or stress?

_____

_____

_____

_____

_____

Applying weighted pressure to your body is known to send a calming signal to your brain. The next time you are feeling stressed or anxious, give yourself a big, tight hug for thirty seconds as you breathe deeply.

**In this moment, I am safe and content.
I feel positive knowing I am secure.**

BE YOUR OWN COACH

Giving yourself love is often easier when you have habits that make it a part of your everyday life. Which of your habits actively support self-love?

_____

_____

_____

_____

_____

_____

_____

Practice this self-love habit each morning for a week: Look at yourself in the mirror and give yourself a pep talk by naming five things you love about yourself.

I actively infuse love into my life with constructive habits and supportive rituals.

MANAGING STRESS LEVELS

If you've ever been overwhelmed or "stressed out," you know that feeling can strain your body. Where do you find that you hold tension in your body when stressed?

_____

_____

_____

_____

_____

_____

_____

Practice this hand massage to help release tension and stress. Gently press one thumb into your other hand as you knead over your palm in a circular direction.

As I breathe deeply, I release stress and tension.

GIVE YOURSELF CREDIT

As you develop more self-love, there is value in acknowledging your improvements. How have you progressed in your self-love journey so far?

_____

_____

_____

_____

_____

_____

Create a self-love tally by tracking your loving thoughts this week. Whenever you notice yourself having a kind thought toward yourself, draw a heart on a piece of paper to represent giving yourself credit.

I love to celebrate my wins. Noticing my progress motivates me to continue.

DON'T DIM YOUR LIGHT

When receiving praise or recognition, many people may use self-deprecation as a defense. Are there ever times you undervalue your worth?

_____

_____

_____

_____

_____

_____

The next time you receive a compliment, practice receiving it without qualifications or self-deprecation. Simply accept the compliment and allow yourself to notice any positive emotions.

**I have tremendous value and embrace
when others celebrate me.**

SHAME, THE OPPOSITE OF LOVE

Sometimes, feeling guilty about something we did can fester into feeling shame about who we are. How can you make amends for something you feel guilty about to support your personal values?

_____

_____

_____

_____

_____

_____

With your eyes closed, become aware of your body. Envision where you feel shame in your body and visualize sending breath to those parts. Inhale, imagine breathing love into those places, and release the shame on the exhale.

**I continue to evolve and better myself.
I am proud of who I am becoming.**

WIRED FOR POSITIVITY

Our brains have evolved to focus on the negative to protect us, so consciously creating positive experiences is a great self-love tactic for balance. What positive experiences do you take for granted that you could be more appreciative of?

_____

_____

_____

_____

_____

Use Dr. Rick Hanson's "Taking in the Good" method to cultivate a positive experience for yourself. Take a good moment, like a sunset, and make it more meaningful by mindfully imagining the good feelings washing over your body.

**I have a positive perspective and
seek out positive experiences.**

INCREASING FEELINGS OF WORTH

There are life experiences that can cause our sense of worth to plummet. Identify these events and define how they don't reflect your value.

_____

_____

_____

_____

_____

_____

Try this value visualization. Start by imagining light simultaneously coming up from your toes and descending from your head. Observe as these lights move to meet at your heart. As you imagine light radiating through you, repeat to yourself, "I am full of loving light."

**I go through life challenges knowing
that I am worthy no matter what.**

BEHOLD YOUR OWN BEAUTY

What are some beautiful things about yourself and how do they help you define beauty?

_____

_____

_____

_____

_____

_____

_____

Create a self-love photo album by assembling photos of things that represent what you love about yourself. Flip through this album whenever you need a self-love boost.

**I am beautiful in many different ways.
I choose to celebrate my beauty.**

AUTHENTICALLY SHOWING UP

In social settings we sometimes try to pretend to be something we aren't due to a lack of confidence. Are you wearing any "masks" in life? How would your life change if you took them off?

_____

_____

_____

_____

_____

_____

Grab a piece of scrap paper and cut it into six to eight small pieces. On each piece, write down any oppressive expectations you feel you have to live up to. Then symbolically free yourself by crumpling each piece of paper and throwing it away.

**I show up in this world in a way that
is authentic to my true self.**

CULTIVATING COURAGE

Loving yourself can look like releasing limiting fears and experiencing freedom. Cultivating courage in this way supports self-kindness because it awakens untapped parts of yourself. What are some fears holding you back?

_____

_____

_____

_____

_____

_____

Use this activity to help face your fears. From the list of fears holding you back, choose one fear and do something this week that will help you face it. Start small and commit to continually releasing this fear.

I can experience freedom by courageously facing my fears and expanding my horizons.

Date: _____

FOSTERING KINDNESS

Sometimes you may place pressure on yourself that causes more harm than good. What is one way you are putting negative pressure on yourself? What could you do to lessen this burden?

_____

_____

_____

_____

_____

_____

Practice this loving-kindness meditation to promote feelings of self-love. Sit quietly and imagine sending love to a friendly acquaintance. Then send love to someone you love. Lastly, imagine sending yourself the same radiating love energy.

I know I am doing my best. I can be kind to myself while still accomplishing my goals.

CONTINUING TO GROW

Honestly taking stock of your life and committing to growth fosters self-confidence as you learn how to nurture your likeable traits. Where in your life would you like to see change in the next year?

_____

_____

_____

_____

_____

_____

Take time this week to expand your horizons and knowledge with activities such as learning a new recipe or begin learning a hobby such as gardening.

I can love myself as I grow. I feel proud as I expand and evolve.

EMPOWERED ACTION FOR CHANGE

On the journey to lovingly improve yourself, it's valuable to name what you can control and resolve not to focus on what you can't. This will help you focus your energy on what truly matters. Reflect on something you want in life. What elements are within your control? Outside of it?

_____

_____

_____

_____

_____

_____

After isolating what you can control, come up with a plan to start taking action in a small way. Make sure to share the plan with a loved one for accountability

I have the power to take actions that bring me closer to what I value.

LIVING ACCORDING TO YOUR PRINCIPLES

Loving yourself is easier when you aren't doing things that don't align with your values. What habits could you quit that don't correspond with the principles that are most important to you?

_____

_____

_____

_____

_____

_____

Choose a new healthy habit and track your ability to maintain this habit for twenty-one days. Note anything that gets in the way of sticking to that routine.

My habits support loving myself. I love doing things that make me feel proud.

PREPARING FOR
SELF-LOVE

Do you ever feel scattered or like you're doing everything at the last minute? This can place us in a frantic state of mind that doesn't feel kind or loving. Evaluate how frantic you feel in life right now. What are the contributing factors?

_____

_____

_____

_____

_____

Do something your future self will thank you for this week. Plan your meals, prepare your clothes, or use an agenda to schedule your time.

**I can do things today that will make
me feel extra loved tomorrow.**

TRUSTING YOUR POSITIVE BELIEFS

Just as many people struggle with negative core beliefs about themselves, most people also have coexisting positive beliefs about themselves. What are some beliefs you have about yourself that refute any negative beliefs?

_____

_____

_____

_____

_____

Using your list, create a positive-belief wheel to post on your wall to review daily. Draw a circle on a piece of paper and divide it into slices like a pie. Within each segment, write a positive belief about yourself. When you struggle with negative thinking, refer to your wheel and read each statement aloud.

I choose to embrace my positive self-beliefs.

LOVING INDULGENCE

When thinking about indulgence, you may be prone to think about unhealthy treats like relying on processed foods or having a drink. In the end, these don't promote self-care. Are there ever times you indulge yourself in ways that don't ultimately serve you?

_____

_____

_____

_____

_____

Engage in a lavish skin care ritual to practice celebrating yourself in a way that feels both indulgent and loving. Light a scented candle and wash your face mindfully using your favorite nourishing skin care products.

I can celebrate myself in ways that nourish me.

NURTURING OURSELVES

There may be ways in which you didn't feel nurtured as a child. In adulthood, you can find ways to give yourself the love you once needed. What parts of yourself or what needs can you tend to now?

_____

_____

_____

_____

_____

_____

_____

Try caring for a new plant or starting a small herb garden. Observe how you are able to care for its needs and take note of how you can apply any nurturing lessons to yourself.

I am empowered to give myself what I need and take care of myself in healing ways.

GIVE YOURSELF REST

Rest is a great tool for self-kindness and compassion. Evaluate your relationship with rest. Do you feel like you must always be productive or busy?

_____

_____

_____

_____

_____

_____

At the end of the week, take any time you can to fully care for yourself in mind, body, and spirit. Whether it's a five-minute mindful shower or an entire self-care Sunday, just do what you can with the intention of allowing yourself rest. See if you can notice any thoughts of resistance without holding on to them, then refocus on caring for yourself.

**I allow myself rest. I allow myself
to pause and feel refreshed.**

START THE DAY WITH LOVE

The beginning of your day can set your mood in motion. Once set, it can be difficult to change throughout the day. Does your typical morning support having a good day?

_____

_____

_____

_____

_____

_____

_____

Practice a five-minute morning routine of stretching, setting an intention for the day, and naming one new thing that you love about yourself.

I start the day with excitement for another opportunity to love myself the way I deserve.

END THE DAY WITH LOVE

The way we close the day also has the power to promote self-love by creating a final opportunity for self-care. What actions can you take that capitalize on this opportunity?

_____

_____

_____

_____

_____

_____

_____

Try a five-minute self-love evening practice that includes decompressing with a small, hot cup of your favorite herbal tea.

Even as the day closes, I am consciously creating opportunities to show myself love.

STEPPING INTO YOUR HIGHER SELF

If you have big goals, it can feel invigorating to envision what it would be like to achieve them. How do you think your life would change if you accomplished your largest goals?

_____

_____

_____

_____

_____

_____

Imagine the highest version of yourself that has accomplished all your dreams. Give a name to this version of yourself and spend tomorrow embodying the energy of this version of yourself.

**Striving for my dreams feels good,
and I am hopeful for my future.**

ACTIVELY SEEKING JOY

Feeling positive emotions like joy can be as simple as intentionally doing activities that bring you joy. Create a list of activities that bring you feelings of joy and excitement.

_____

_____

_____

_____

_____

_____

_____

Offer yourself joy by scheduling three activities from your list to complete in the next three days.

I have power over the way I feel. I bring joy into my emotional experience.

BECOMING LESS JUDGMENTAL

Discovering the roots of your inner judgment gives you the power to address them. When and how did you develop your self-judgmental thoughts?

_____

_____

_____

_____

_____

_____

Foster a nonjudgmental perspective with this thought meditation. Close your eyes and breathe deeply as you notice arising thoughts. For five minutes, practice observing thoughts without judging them. Gently release each thought and focus on noticing the next arising thought.

I love myself a little more the less judgmental I become.

ENVISIONING WHAT'S ON THE HORIZON

Self-love includes having high hopes for yourself. These high hopes cultivate motivation and inspiration to propel you forward. Do you believe that you can create a meaningful, valuable life for yourself? Why or why not?

_____

_____

_____

_____

_____

_____

Create a collage that encompasses the vision you have for your life. Include pictures and clippings that represent a grand life full of self-love.

My future is bright, and I have high hopes for myself.

TRY SOMETHING NEW

Attempting something new fosters confidence because you must trust yourself to adapt in new situations. How do you feel when you try new things? Do any fears get in the way?

_____

_____

_____

_____

_____

_____

_____

Expand your passions by beginning a new hobby. Make sure this endeavor is something you have never done to ensure novelty is a part of your experience.

I trust myself to figure out new things and situations. Everything can be figured out.

SOCIAL MEDIA BREAK

You've likely heard of the many negative impacts social media can have on our self-esteem. What are your own personal signs that social media is negatively impacting you?

_____

_____

_____

_____

_____

_____

_____

Take a one-week social media break. During this week, notice what emotions and thoughts arise during the day and how you feel at the end of the day.

Taking breaks to care for myself is good for my well-being. I will prioritize my joy.

Date: _____

CONNECTING IN REAL LIFE

Connection allows you to confidently put yourself out there and
fulfill one of your basic human needs. How would you evaluate
your ability to put yourself out there to connect with others?

_____

_____

_____

_____

_____

_____

Join a new group to increase your socialization in real life. Search
groups to join on meetup sites and social sites, but ultimately
attend an in-person meeting to foster connection.

**Connecting with others helps me feel
loved and seen. I nurture connections
that make me feel good.**

INTERIOR WELL-BEING

Creating a space that supports your unique style, creativity, and joy can be a great way to cultivate self-love, because our environments can drastically impact our mood. What elements within your own home foster wellness?

_____

_____

_____

_____

_____

Pick a place in your home that could use a boost of inspiration and intentionality. Then take time to creatively add elements to the space that would make it more joyful and represent your individuality. Consider adding aromatherapy, plants, art, or displays of memories or proud achievements.

I intentionally create spaces around me to support loving myself to the fullest potential.

CLEAR YOUR MIND

Clutter has a way of overstimulating us even when we're not paying attention to it. As such, decluttering can be a great way to create a more calming and loving environment for yourself. What areas of your home gather clutter easily?

_____

_____

_____

_____

_____

_____

_____

Set a ten-minute timer to declutter a space. Start with tossing the trash. Then organize items that belong in other areas. Then simply tidy the remaining items in the area.

**My environment supports my
tranquility and calmness.**

THE ANTICIPATION
OF IT ALL

Looking forward to something in the future can bring about excitement and anticipation by giving you ways to feel alive and purposeful. What was the last thing you were really excited about?

_____

_____

_____

_____

_____

_____

Get excited for the future by planning your "bucket list" for the next few months. A bucket list is a list of activities you hope to do in this lifetime.

I look forward to experiencing more joy.

GIVING LOVE TO OTHERS

Helping others can alleviate overly focusing on ourselves and emphasize the blessings and privilege within our own lives. What are some of your favorite ways to give to others?

_____

_____

_____

_____

_____

_____

This week, try to shift your focus by doing something like volunteering, donating gently used items, or giving to the community. Notice what feelings arise as you help others.

Helping others fills me with light and helps me reach new depths of my purpose.

PLEASURE AS
SELF-COMPASSION

Sometimes we can forget to prioritize fun as we try to manage all our responsibilities. Pleasure is a valuable way to give yourself a more balanced experience in life. What was the most fun thing you've done in the last year?

_____

_____

_____

_____

_____

_____

Grab a friend and go out with the sole purpose of having fun. See if you can include activities on your outing that will make you laugh or experience adventure.

I feel lighter when I laugh and have fun.
I allow myself the pleasure I deserve.

PURSUE YOUR DREAMS

Many find it helpful to connect their goals to their purpose to inspire action. If your biggest goals and dreams came true, how would this allow you to fulfill your life's purpose?

_____

_____

_____

_____

_____

_____

Close your eyes and breathe deeply. Contemplate what your dreams were when you were a child. Connect with how you felt hoping for these dreams and why you wanted to achieve them.

**My dreams inspire me to fulfill
my purpose in new ways.**

DEALING WITH UNWANTED THOUGHTS

Some of the negative thoughts we have about ourselves are intrusive, unwanted, and can feel like they pop into your head out of nowhere. Do you struggle with any recurring intrusive thoughts that affect your self-esteem?

_____

_____

_____

_____

_____

The next time you experience an unwanted intrusive thought, pause and place your hand on your heart. Imagine sending yourself love and think of three statements that refute that thought.

Many negative thoughts are either untrue or unhelpful. I can choose to focus on new thoughts.

GIVE YOURSELF FREE TIME

If you are frequently hard on yourself, you may falsely assume that you must always be working or productive. Can you recall moments when you weren't working that you felt angst?

_____

_____

_____

_____

_____

_____

Take a moment to plan your week ahead. While scheduling priority tasks and meetings each day, block time in your schedule to do whatever you want outside of work.

I don't have to be hard on myself, because I know my worth is not dependent on my work.

LET YOUR CREATIVITY FLOW

Creativity is known to help reduce stress and foster peace. Too often, though, it takes a back seat as we work toward fulfilling our responsibilities. How would you evaluate the amount of time you spend being creative?

_____

_____

_____

_____

_____

_____

The next time you are working, build in a fifteen-minute creativity break. Use this time to work on any creative endeavor that brings you joy, such as doodling, coloring, writing a story, or even taking photos.

Aligning with my inner creativity allows me to express my true self without judgment.

LOVE DEEPLY

When you begin to fully accept yourself, it opens doors to love others more deeply, and, just as important, it allow others to love you as well. Do you allow yourself to experience love in a profound way?

_____

_____

_____

_____

_____

Think of someone you love. Make a basket of admiration to express your love for them. Fill it with five things that will bring them joy such as a favorite candy, an affirming note, or even a picture of the two of you.

Experiencing trusting and safe love is my right. I relish the abundance of love that surrounds me.

LAUGHTER AND LOVE

Laughter has the power to make us feel alive and happy. Being intentional about laughing more and experiencing pleasure is a great way to show yourself love. What are the situations in which you find yourself laughing the most?

_____

_____

_____

_____

_____

_____

Mindfully watch a funny movie or show. Notice what emotions arise and the way your body feels as you experience pleasure. Take note of any thoughts, feelings, or sensations that arise afterward as well.

I will be intentional about laughing more, having fun, and allowing myself joy.

SWEET SATISFACTION

Some struggle with self-love because, deep down, they don't feel like they deserve love. Are there times in your life when you are too hard on yourself?

_____

_____

_____

_____

_____

_____

Think about a goal that you have. Set mini goals that will help you achieve this larger goal. For each milestone you achieve, reward yourself with a small treat. Allow yourself to feel the satisfaction of rewarding yourself.

**I will seek opportunities to praise myself.
I know I deserve love and admiration.**

SUSTAINABLE HUSTLE

Burnout is a common experience within our culture. Our demanding, fast-paced world doesn't account for our natural human limitations. Is your current work-life balance sustainable?

_____

_____

_____

_____

_____

_____

_____

Take a moment to plan your day tomorrow. Focus on realistic expectations for your time and energy. If possible, try to include a one-hour buffer in your schedule that will allow for overflow and breaks.

If am more conscious of my natural limitations, I can intentionally offer myself grace.

SEE YOURSELF AS SUCCESSFUL

Defining success in a self-compassionate way can help you lean into more abundance in your current life instead of making your joy conditional on some future achievement. How can you define success in a way that makes you already feel successful right now in your life?

_____

_____

_____

_____

_____

Make a list of all the successes that you are proud of, big or small, right now in your life. Then write each success on a sticky note to place on your mirror and read them daily for one week.

I am successful in my own right. I am trying my best and constantly moving forward.

IT WAS ALL A DREAM

Taking time to be present reveals that blessings are all around. This is a great form of self-compassion because it focuses your thoughts on positivity. How much of your current reality was once just dreams?

_____

_____

_____

_____

_____

_____

Make an appreciation board by decorating a poster board with images of things that you have already manifested, achieved, or received.

I luxuriate in the blessings that were once dreams. Abundance surrounds me.

STOP DOUBTING YOURSELF

If you struggle with self-doubt, you may notice that if you take action even while doubting yourself, you usually rise to the occasion and quell any doubts. Reflect on times when you didn't trust yourself but still accomplished what you set out to do.

_____

_____

_____

_____

_____

_____

The next time you find yourself struggling with self-doubt, take a moment to visualize what it would look like to fully trust yourself. Then commit to doing one thing to embody this type of self-trust.

Fears and doubts may come, but I can choose to carry them with me as I pursue my values anyway.

BE HONEST WITH YOURSELF

Integrity means doing the right thing even when others aren't looking. As such, integrity serves as a route to fully seeing the person within. In what areas of your life could you be more honest with yourself?

_____

_____

_____

_____

Referring to today's journal entry, pick an area of your life that could use more self-discipline. This week, take one small step toward improving in this area.

I can make an honest assessment of my areas for improvement with love, compassion, and a commitment to evolving.

YOUR OWN WORST ENEMY

Self-sabotage is the devastating phenomenon of unintentionally harming yourself with counterproductive thoughts and behaviors. Have there been times you have gotten in the way of your own happiness?

_____

_____

_____

_____

_____

Use this exercise to practice self-love the next time you notice yourself doing something that isn't in your best interest. Pause and begin deep breathing. Imagine inhaling all the goodness you deserve. On each exhale, relax your body a little more.

I affirm my right to success and happiness. I will get out of my own way in my self-love journey.

WHEN FEELING UNMOTIVATED...

Low motivation can have a crushing effect on your journey to living a confident life. Can you recall times when low motivation affected your confidence in yourself?

_____

_____

_____

_____

_____

_____

_____

Identify a song that motivates you and makes you feel energized. The next time you're feeling sluggish and uninspired, play this song and dance!

**I have the power to pull myself out of funks
by starting small and being kind to myself.**

FEELING SAFE AND SUPPORTED

If it's difficult for you to see the world as a safe and supportive space, it may impact your ability to fully allow yourself to expand and take risks. Are there ways you hold back in life because you don't trust the world?

_____

_____

_____

_____

_____

Think of any fears you have of putting yourself out there in the world. Practice safe vulnerability by sharing with a trusted friend how you will face this fear.

I am empowered to create safe spaces and connections that support my expansion.

AMPLIFY YOUR PLEASURE

Connecting in the moment with your day-to-day pleasures can turn the mundane into the miraculous. What are the simple things in life that bring you substantial joy?

_____

_____

_____

_____

_____

_____

Offer yourself love throughout the day today by acknowledging small miracles. When you notice something joyful, embrace the moment by noticing your emotions, your thoughts, and all your senses.

**I deserve to enjoy my life to the fullest
with pleasure and peace.**

FIND THE RIGHT
NORTH STAR

If you are led by what others think of you, you are on a road of unrealistic expectations and emptiness. Are you holding yourself back in any ways due to fear of judgment?

_____

_____

_____

_____

_____

_____

Do one thing this week that you've always wanted to do but haven't because you were afraid of what people might think. If it's something big, break it down into one small action you could take to start.

**I don't live my life to impress others.
Impressing myself is my goal.**

RECEIVE YOUR WORTH

It doesn't serve us to go through life accepting less than we deserve. Are there domains in your life where you don't feel properly valued?

_____

_____

_____

_____

_____

_____

The next time you feel undervalued, use assertive communication to declare your worth. Do this by owning how you feel and sharing what you need directly and empathetically. Decide what would make you feel valued, and express that need to whom it may concern.

I have the power to ask for what I deserve.

YOU CAN EVOLVE

Personal development is possible through self-knowledge and discipline. In what ways are you committed to becoming a better person?

_____

_____

_____

_____

_____

_____

_____

Sit quietly and close your eyes. Imagine you are a seed being planted in the soil. Envision that seed growing from sprout to flower and notice how you feel as you watch it flourish.

I commit to prospering, flourishing, and thriving. Bettering myself allows me to reach my highest potential.

GOOD THINGS
HAPPEN TO YOU

One very common negative core belief that erodes self-love is the idea that you are destined for disappointment. Do you ever have thoughts that may be fueled by the belief that good things don't happen for you?

_____

_____

_____

_____

_____

_____

Take a good things outing. On this outing, notice things that you would like to have in your life, such as a nice car you see or a loving moment you witness. Afterward, imagine having these things for yourself.

I deserve good things. I believe good things are easily flowing into my life.

STOP DISQUALIFYING THE POSITIVITY

Low self-esteem may cause you to disqualify the positive. Have you ever caught yourself downplaying one of your achievements? Do you feel uncomfortable with success?

_____

_____

_____

_____

_____

When you notice yourself focusing on the negative, make a two-column list on a piece of paper. On the left side, note all the positive things about this situation; on the right side, list all the negative things. Then fold the paper so that you only see the positives and read the list aloud.

I will allow myself to fully indulge in the positive aspects of myself and life.

TAPPING INTO PASSION

Passion is an intense experience of joy, satisfaction, and pleasure. Finding more ways to experience passion is a powerful way to practice self-care because it fulfills your inherent desires. What are you most passionate about in life?

_____

_____

_____

_____

_____

_____

Make a promise to yourself to do something you are passionate about this week. Revisit your favorites—a book, ice cream flavor, or even a hobby from childhood.

**I have the space and freedom to lean
into passions and fill myself up.**

LOVING YOURSELF FULLY

Imagine the power of fully knowing and accepting yourself with kindness and compassion. How would your life change if you fully loved yourself?

_____

_____

_____

_____

_____

Create a collage of five pictures that represent the life you envisioned in today's prompt. For one week, look at this collage daily and use the phrase "I am" followed by five words that represent the essence of your optimal self-love life.

**I embody the ultimate vision of self-love
by intentionally cultivating grace,
compassion, and acceptance for myself.**

FRESH PERSPECTIVE

A willingness to be wrong and try new things opens up pathways for your expansion. Have you struggled with embracing change?

_____

_____

_____

_____

_____

_____

The next time you feel you are rushing to dismiss a new idea, pause and take a moment to reflect on what may be possible. Try to expand your perspective by discussing the new idea with someone else before dismissing it.

**I am open to new possibilities with
the potential to help me grow.**

KEEP GOING

One of the greatest disservices we can do to ourselves is to give up on important goals. Are there any goals you have stopped working toward that you would find value in picking up again?

_____

_____

_____

_____

_____

_____

Think of a friend or loved one who would be a great accountability partner. Share your goals with each other and commit to checking in with each other about your progress.

Persevering as I strive toward my goals is an act of love. It helps me reach my potential and experience satisfaction.

DEVELOP RESILIENCY

A great way to foster perseverance is by developing resiliency. This is a character trait that prescribes making meaning from our challenges in order to evolve. What are some situations in which you found meaning in a life challenge and resiliently kept going during a difficult time?

_____

_____

_____

_____

_____

Use this activity to develop resiliency. Dedicate a special notebook to meaningful experiences. Anytime you recognize a life lesson, add it to this notebook. Read back through your experiences anytime life feels challenging.

Life obstacles are opportunities to give myself grace and kindness while learning beneficial lessons.

PLAN AHEAD

Prior planning is a great organizational tool for self-compassion. What areas of your life would benefit from more planning?

_____

_____

_____

_____

_____

_____

_____

_____

Think of a regular occurrence or task in your life that you dread doing. Then do things ahead of time to prepare for that next task that will make it more bearable in the future.

**I can organize my life in ways that
make it easier for me to thrive.**

CREATE SYSTEMS
FOR YOUR GOALS

Goals are great. Goals with systems and plans to achieve those goals are better. What systems would support the current goals you have in place?

_____

_____

_____

_____

_____

_____

Pick one of the systems you identified above and decide on a habit that would support this plan. For the next month, develop this positive habit.

**When I focus on what I can control,
I set myself up for success.**

SAY NO MORE OFTEN

It's easy to think that going out of your way to make others happy will lead to your own happiness. However, people-pleasing can often inversely impact self-kindness. Learning to say no more often may be the most valuable tool in your self-love toolbox. Do you ever fall into a people-pleasing mode?

_____

_____

_____

_____

_____

When you notice the urge to say yes to someone in a situation that does not serve you, use the SUN formula: Stop. Unapologetically say no. Nicely redirect them to other resources.

It's not my job to please everybody all the time. My happiness is just as important as others'.

HABIT STACKING

Every day presents an opportunity to love yourself. What habits do you have that support self-love and self-care?

_____

_____

_____

_____

_____

_____

_____

Author James Clear popularized the concept of habit stacking, where new habits build upon the old ones by adding an action to the end of an existing behavior. Each time you brush your teeth this week, follow it with "I love myself because" and fill in the blank.

I find ways to fill my life with actions of love.

KIND SELF-TALK

You've hopefully learned by now that much of the work to love ourselves more begins with our thoughts and how we talk to ourselves. Over the last week, can you recall any times you used positive self-talk to combat negativity?

_____

_____

_____

_____

_____

Asking yourself questions is a great strategy to reframe negative thoughts into positive ones. The next time you experience a self-critical thought (such as "I am so stupid") ask yourself, "What are three reasons I am actually (insert the opposite of the critical thought, such as "smart")?" and answer aloud.

**I can influence my unconscious to
be more loving and kind.**

FEELING WARM AND FUZZY

For many, offering love to others can be an act of self-compassion because they feel so fulfilled making other people feel good. How do you make your loved ones feel special?

_____

_____

_____

_____

_____

_____

Each night this week, share something with a loved one that you love about them. You can make it a reciprocal practice and enjoy a moment celebrating each other's goodness each day.

**Offering love to others is offering
myself more love, too.**

FILL UP YOUR CUP

Sometimes a little boost of motivation can go a long way. What are some encouraging phrases that make you feel uplifted?

_____

_____

_____

_____

_____

_____

_____

_____

Each morning for the next week, write down a motivational quote on a piece of paper, fold it, and put it in a cup. At the end of the week, empty the cup and read what you found moving.

I am constantly filling myself up with encouragement and motivation.

CELEBRATE YOUR UNIQUENESS

Embracing your uniqueness and differences is an excellent method of self-acceptance. What are your unique traits that you love?

_____

_____

_____

_____

_____

_____

This activity will help you put your differences on display to be celebrated! In a small box, place items that represent what makes you you and then share this box with a loved one.

**I am a unique individual. I love
what makes me different.**

SHARE YOUR STORY

Having a narrative of your own journey and triumphs can make life meaningful. This is because reflecting on your life with a perspective that accounts for lessons and growth helps make sense of the larger picture of your life. What are the biggest triumphs that highlight your life?

_____

_____

_____

_____

_____

_____

_____

Write a short story of your life last week. Make sure you are the hero of your story and describe a beginning, obstacle that you overcame, and conclusion.

My story has meaning and value.

EMBRACING OBSTACLES

I hope I have instilled within you the importance of learning from life challenges in order to love yourself through them. Are there life stressors that you are facing that you can evaluate for lessons?

_____

_____

_____

_____

_____

_____

_____

Use this visualization to help yourself cope with any current life stressors. Envision coming out of the other side of this dilemma with a new perspective and new skills. See yourself overcoming this obstacle and experiencing relief.

**I honor the tension of change. I know
it is an opportunity to evolve.**

LEARN LESSONS ONCE

In braving challenges, sometimes the lesson doesn't quite stick on the first try. Has there ever been a time where you found it hard to apply past life lessons?

_____

_____

_____

_____

_____

_____

_____

When you encounter a problem, take some time to connect with nature. While experiencing more groundedness, breathe deeply and think of any life lessons that may help in this situation before returning to problem-solving.

**I honor the lessons of the past
as I embrace my future.**

SOCIAL MEDIA
WELLNESS PLAN

Social media gives us a look into the lives of people we might never encounter, but it's important to remember that what people post is cultivated for an audience. What aspects of social media impact your self-esteem?

_____

_____

_____

_____

_____

_____

While taking breaks is useful, having an intentional way of using social media is also helpful. Develop a wellness plan for how you will use social media to ensure your mental well-being.

**I breathe deeply and own my power to
use technology for my benefit.**

COMPASSION AS YOU GROW

It can be tricky to accept yourself while also tasking yourself with the responsibility to change for the better. How do you accept your limitations with compassion while committing to evolve?

_____

_____

_____

_____

_____

_____

Think of something about yourself that you struggling to change. Divide a sheet of paper into quadrants. In the top two quadrants, write the pros and cons of changing. In the bottom quadrants, write the pros and cons of not making this change.

I have compassion for my limitations and know I am doing my best.

INTENTIONALLY LIVING AND LOVING

Assigning intentions to your actions is a way to step into your power. How intentional is your life now? Do you feel like you are living life on purpose?

_____

_____

_____

_____

_____

_____

Set an intention for each segment of your day tomorrow: morning, afternoon, and evening. Before going to bed, notice how these intentions shaped your day.

I am the creator of my life. I offer myself love by living a life on my own terms.

ADVOCATING FOR YOUR NEEDS

Many people feel the pressure to be self-sufficient and struggle to assert their needs. Are there times you unknowingly sacrifice yourself by not asking for help?

_____

_____

_____

_____

_____

_____

This activity will help you get into the habit of asking for help. In the next few days, anytime you have a task or challenge, find a way to ask someone for help even if you think you should be able to figure it out on your own.

**I am my own best advocate. I joyously
receive the help I need.**

SEE YOURSELF HAPPY

Our language impacts how we feel about ourselves. Making the shift to view yourself as a happy person can support your self-love journey. How would you describe a happy person?

_____

_____

_____

_____

_____

_____

_____

Stare into a mirror smiling for one minute. As you smile at yourself, imagine embodying all the traits you described in today's prompt.

**I am fully capable of experiencing happiness.
I love seeing myself as a happy person.**

ASSESS YOUR JOURNEY

Any growth journey is aided by tracking because it helps you progress. As you continue your journey to more self-love, how will you evaluate your growth?

_____

_____

_____

_____

_____

_____

_____

On a sheet of paper, make a visual representation of the self-love path you've taken since starting this journal. Along your path, note various milestones that helped you move forward and increase your self-love.

I am committed to the journey and value the practice, not only the destination.

REFRAMING DEFICITS

I hope this last prompt inspires you to continue embracing every part of your beautiful, authentic self. Think of your personal deficits and use this space to consider how you could reframe them into something positive, something that empowers you to embrace every single part of yourself.

_____

_____

_____

_____

_____

Pretend you are giving a speech. As you introduce yourself, imagine introducing someone acclaimed by restructuring all of your weaknesses into strengths.

I love myself unconditionally. Everything about me is worth celebrating, because even my flaws make me who I am.